LONDON ON FIRE

A Great City at the time of the Great Fire

John C. Miles

London on Fire!

It began with a Small Thing, as many Big Things do. After a hot day baking on a baking hot day in 1666, Thomas Farrinor went to bed. Perhaps he was tired, careless; perhaps it was easy for him to miss one small red-hot ember. Whatever happened, in a few hours his bakery near London Bridge was alight. Farrinor couldn't have known, as he leaped from his bed to shouts of 'Fire!' that more than 13,000 houses, as well as churches, public buildings and a great cathedral were doomed.

The Great Fire of London has gone down in history as one of the most dreadful events to befall an early modern city in peacetime. But to get a sense of what was swept away, we need to examine what was there before. So this book begins not with a narrative of the fire, but with events leading up to the Restoration of the monarchy and a look at what life in London was like in the years 1660–1666. After the Great Fire, we move away from the destruction to other parts of London, including those that were to be developed in the years following, giving a glimpse of how those momentous few days in September 1666 helped lay the foundations of London as the modern city we know today. The whole book celebrates a city that was on fire with new ideas and burning with potential.

Contents

Welcome to London

Welcome to a bustling city filled with people and packed with buildings, life and colour. It is a place where the rich in their enormous houses and the poor sleeping rough rub shoulders every day. As you walk along a street, you hear men and women speaking many different languages. There are lots of new arrivals – visitors and migrants looking for work.

This is London today, right? Well, yes it is, but it also describes London in the 1660s.

This map shows London in 1658. It was a much smaller place than today. At the centre was the City of London, founded 1,500 years earlier by the Romans and still partially defined by its medieval walls.

Westward ran Fleet Street, the Strand and the newly developed area of Covent Garden. Then London petered out beyond Charing Cross, Whitehall and Westminster with open fields and market gardens – today, London's 'West End'.

Then and now

Of course, there were no cars, trains, electricity, planes or computers in 1660s London. If we could travel back in time, many things would seem unfamiliar, but others might seem much the same as today. It was still a crowded city. People worked hard, fell in love, raised children, became ill, died and were buried. They had many of the same hopes and dreams that we do.

A great city

This book gives a picture of London life in the 1660s – from the time of the Restoration (see page 6) through to the Great Fire of 1666 and the London that emerged from the ashes. Much of it is arranged area by area, like a travel guide, so you can imagine exploring the city then – and go and see some of the sights that are still standing today.

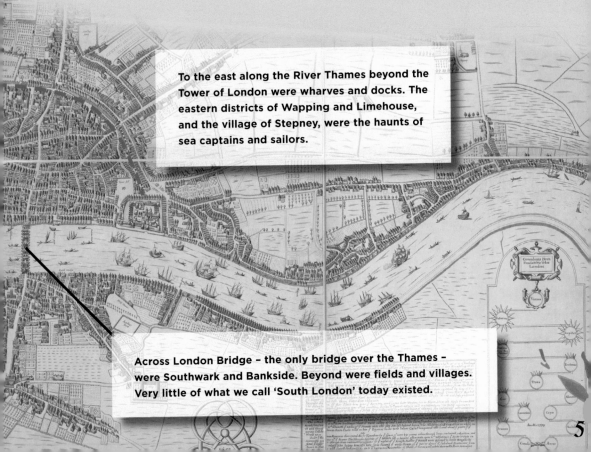

To the east along the River Thames beyond the Tower of London were wharves and docks. The eastern districts of Wapping and Limehouse, and the village of Stepney, were the haunts of sea captains and sailors.

Across London Bridge – the only bridge over the Thames – were Southwark and Bankside. Beyond were fields and villages. Very little of what we call 'South London' today existed.

Restoration!

In 1660 something exciting happened – King Charles II, who had been living in exile in the Netherlands, was invited to return to Britain and take his place as king. This event is known as 'the Restoration' because the monarchy was 'restored' to Britain. But why had Charles been living abroad in the first place?

Cromwell, wounded, rides into battle on a white horse at Marston Moor, 1644.

Civil wars

Throughout the 1640s Britain experienced a terrible series of civil wars fought between supporters of King Charles I and those of Parliament. What Britons were fighting about was mainly who had the right to govern, and how. The King's supporters believed that the monarch had the right to rule from God. Supporters of Parliament believed that a king should rule alongside elected members of Parliament (MPs), or that Parliament alone should rule, without a king.

Death of the King

After many battles over a number of years, forces loyal to King Charles I were defeated by the forces of Parliament led by Oliver Cromwell, who then governed Britain as 'Lord Protector' of a 'Commonwealth' with the help of Parliament. King Charles I was put on trial and beheaded in London on 30 January 1649.

Religion and daily life

In the 17th century, nearly everyone went to church and prayed to God daily. England's official Christian Church was the Protestant Church of England, founded by King Henry VIII in 1534–36 when he rejected Roman Catholicism and the authority of the Pope in Rome. Roman Catholics now were regarded with suspicion as possible spies and traitors.

Different Protestant groups had arisen within the Church, each with their own ideas about the best way to worship God. One group, the so-called 'Puritans', dressed plainly, rejected elaborate religious ceremonies and spent many hours in prayer. Oliver Cromwell was Puritan and under his rule, churches were stripped of their decorations, theatres were closed and traditional religious festivals such as Christmas were banned.

Return of the King

When Oliver Cromwell died in 1658, his son Richard took over. But Richard lacked support and soon King Charles II, the son of Charles I, was invited by Parliament to return from exile in the Netherlands. Charles now ruled with the help of Parliament. Most of the country rejoiced as the long years of war. the Commonwealth and austerity were finally over.

Charles II parades triumphantly through London on his return in 1660.

The City of London

In the 1660s London was booming as thousands of people flooded in looking for jobs created by the return of King Charles and his court. There were lots of opportunities to get on in life and to make money – many of which were in the City of London.

Why 'the City'?

The 'City of London' refers to the historic heart of the capital, surrounded on three sides by walls, and gates that could be shut for defence. By the 1660s London's walls were mostly redundant, and houses spilled out into what had been the fields beyond. However the City of London retained its own system of local government led by the Lord Mayor, and guarded its own traditions.

Organising the City

The City was organised into parishes, each with its own stone-built church, around which houses crowded in narrow lanes and streets. Parish officials looked after the poor and policed the streets. Every citizen 'belonged' to a parish, which was partly responsible for his or her welfare.

"London,

Tall London houses maximised the space available.

Narrow streets

Most streets in the City were narrow and crowded with people, carts and animals. In some places tall houses on either side of the street almost met at the top, making the roadway below very dark. Major roads, such as Cheapside and Thames Street, were wider and allowed more vehicles to pass, but jams caused by overturned carts and heavy traffic were common.

Samuel Pepys – man of London

Samuel Pepys, the son of a tailor, was born in 1633. A civil servant – he helped to run the Navy – Pepys kept a diary from 1660–1669. His detailed entries focus on home life, relationships with his wife and family, work, festivals and, most memorably, vivid accounts of the Great Plague and Great Fire. His diary is one of the most important sources of what we know about London life in the 1660s. Pepys died in 1703.

The diarist and naval administrator Samuel Pepys, painted by John Hayls in 1666.

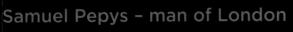

" thou art the flower of cities all! "

William Dunbar (1465–1520)

London housing

Most London houses were built of timber (wood) frames and were up to five storeys high. Bricks or a lattice of sticks covered with plaster filled the spaces between the timbers. Each storey projected beyond the one below to allow larger rooms upstairs. The wealthiest London merchants lived in huge houses built of stone – palaces in all but name.

Food, cooking and lighting

There were no supermarkets or refrigerators. You would have bought food daily from London's many markets. Some of these, such as Leadenhall Market, survive today. Londoners lit their homes with candles; for heating and cooking they relied on open fires. Open flames were dangerous in wooden-framed houses, and the risk of fire was ever-present.

The 1660s

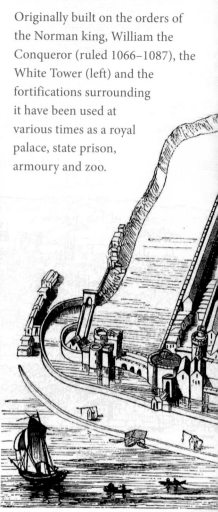

Originally built on the orders of the Norman king, William the Conqueror (ruled 1066–1087), the White Tower (left) and the fortifications surrounding it have been used at various times as a royal palace, state prison, armoury and zoo.

By the 1660s the Tower of London had fallen into disrepair. Kings and queens traditionally travelled in a procession from the Tower to Westminster Abbey for their coronation ceremony. Charles II was the last monarch to do this, in April 1661. But the Tower of London was so uncomfortable that he didn't stay there the night before, as was customary.

Prison and execution

The Tower had acted as a prison for hundreds of years. In the early 1660s it held some of the regicides – those officials who had condemned King Charles I to death in 1649. They were found guilty of the murder of the King and executed.

Public executions took place on Tower Hill, close by the Tower. Prisoners guilty of treason were taken to a scaffold to be hung, drawn and quartered. First, each prisoner was briefly hung by

the neck. They were then cut down whilst still alive and the executioner ripped out their guts. Finally each body was beheaded and chopped into four parts. These, along with the head, were displayed in public places to act as a warning to other potential traitors.

> ❝ To dinner to my Lady Sandwich, and Sir Thomas Crew's children coming thither, I took them and all my Ladys to the Tower and showed them the lions and all that was to be shown. ❞
>
> Samuel Pepys, 3 May 1662

Crown Jewels

The Tower of London had kept the Crown Jewels safe since the 1200s. But in 1649 Cromwell's government melted down or sold the crowns and other precious items. They had to be quickly recreated for the coronation of King Charles II.

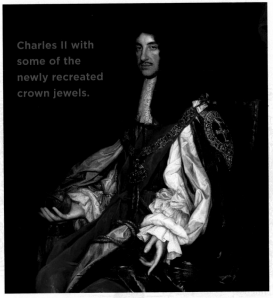

Charles II with some of the newly recreated crown jewels.

The Royal Menagerie

The Royal Menagerie, or zoo, was also at the Tower of London. At various times it had been home to a wine-drinking elephant and a polar bear that delighted Londoners by catching fish in the Thames. You could go to the menagerie and see the lions housed in the 'Lion Tower'. To avoid paying the entrance fee, you could bring along a dog or a cat to be fed to the lions instead.

The Tower of London

In the eastern part of the City of London sits London's fortress, the Tower of London. Its central structure, the White Tower, has stood for more than nine hundred years.

WEST.

A view of Cheapside in the late 1500s. The water conduit (see next page) is next to the church, on the right.

The Heart of the City

Cheapside was one of the City of London's most important streets, wider and grander than most other roadways. It took its name from the medieval English word 'cheap', which meant a marketplace.

The City's high street

Cheapside was a bustling, busy place, alive with noise, colour and smells. You would see the houses of important merchants and shops selling luxury goods. Markets in and around Cheapside provided Londoners with all kinds of food.

The Guildhall

Near Cheapside stood the Guildhall. Dating from the 1400s, the Guildhall was an important building, from where the Lord Mayor and his officials ran the City. Its huge medieval hall (above) was used for official banquets and famous legal trials.

The Guilds

The City of London's Guilds, or 'livery companies', regulated the trades carried on there. For example, the Worshipful Company of Grocers controlled the spice trade, the Fishmongers the selling of fish, the Mercers the general merchants, and so on. The Guilds permitted you to trade and ensured that the goods you sold were of high quality.

Most livery companies had their own halls (headquarters) in the City of London, where they admitted new members and carried on business. The hall of the most important guild, the Mercers, was just off Cheapside.

Livery companies helped look after their members, who voted each year to elect the new Lord Mayor and other City of London officials. Each livery company also took part in the annual procession of the newly elected Lord Mayor.

The Royal Exchange

Not far from Cheapside, the Royal Exchange was a place where merchants met to make deals. It was built by Sir Thomas Gresham, an important 16th-century merchant, and was opened by Queen Elizabeth I in 1571.

The Royal Exchange, by the artist Wenceslaus Hollar. Merchants stroll and deal in the courtyard.

Water supply

A man-made river, the Great Conduit, brought fresh water into the heart of the City of London. Built in the medieval period, the conduit ran from the Tyburn, a river northwest of London, to a building on Cheapside. Here Londoners collected water in barrels. Elsewhere, buried pipes made of elm wood carried water to homes. Holes could be made in the pipes to fight nearby fires.

Old St Paul's

High above the river in the middle of the City of London, old St Paul's Cathedral dominated London's skyline for more than four hundred years.

Roman Catholic old St Paul's survived the religious changes of the 1530s to become the main church of the Anglican Bishop of London. It combined Norman-style architecture, with its rounded arches, and the newer Gothic style, which had pointed arches. St Paul's was massive, at more than 175 m long.

Spire disaster

St Paul's was topped by a soaring 150-m-high spire for more than 200 years. But the spire was struck by lightning during a terrible storm in 1561. It collapsed and set the roof on fire. The cathedral never really recovered from this disaster – cracked by the heat of the fire, its stone walls became weakened.

Old St Paul's resembled a huge ship sailing over London's rooftops.

What's in a word?

The word 'cathedral' comes from the Latin word *cathedra*, which means 'seat'. A cathedral contains the seat – the ceremonial throne – of a bishop. It is the main church in the diocese – the area for which he or she is responsible.

Queene hythe

Inigo Jones steps in

King Charles II's father, Charles I, was unhappy about the state of old St Paul's. He raised more than £100,000 – a huge sum – and asked his favourite architect, Inigo Jones (see page 20), to repair the building. Jones, who was a fan of all things Italian, rebuilt part of the cathedral and added a rather wacky porch (see below). But there was still more to do.

Commonwealth destruction

During Oliver Cromwell's time in power (see pages 6–7) old St Paul's suffered more neglect. Seen by Puritans as a symbol of the Roman Catholics they hated, Cromwell's army officers stabled their horses inside. By the 1660s the once impressive building was in a sorry state.

Rebuilding St Paul's

After the Restoration, King Charles set up a committee to see what could be done to repair or rebuild old St Paul's. A young Oxford professor, Christopher Wren (1632–1723), was one of its members. He had some radical ideas, including replacing the spire with a vast dome. Some committee members weren't convinced, but by the end of August 1666 most supported Wren's plans.

The 3. Cranes

People met and gossiped inside old St Paul's vast interior.

15

West of the bridge

West of London Bridge, the north side of the river was lined with warehouses crowded around docks such as Queenhithe. Narrow streets like Dowgate Hill and Garlick Hill connected the river to Thames Street and Cannon Street, two of the City's main east-west roads.

Unloading goods

Riverside warehouses allowed workers to easily unload goods from small boats called lighters. In a world lit only by candles and lanterns, the risk of fire was high, as these timber-framed buildings were packed with all kinds of flammable material – leather, tar, cooking oil, alcohol and wood were just some of them.

A famous view of London by the Dutch artist Claes Visscher, 1616.

Along the Thames

The Lord Mayor's procession

Every year the City of London staged a grand procession along the River Thames. This was led by the Lord Mayor, who was rowed in his golden state barge (official boat). The Lord Mayor's barge was followed by the decorated barges of many of the livery companies, as well as hundreds of smaller craft. Banners streamed in the wind and musicians played as the procession moved along. People crowded the banks of the river, hung out of windows or took to boats themselves to watch this colourful spectacle.

St Magnus

The river had only one bridge then: London Bridge (see pages 34–35) at the foot of Fish Street Hill. It was lined with houses and shops and the Church of St Magnus stood at its northern end. Carts and other traffic rumbled past its west door during services.

Billingsgate fish market

East of St Magnus you would have smelled a fishy smell in the air, and heard the shouts of market traders. This was Billingsgate Dock, the site of London's biggest fish market. Fish was an important food in the diet of Londoners in the 1660s. Many days in the Church's yearly calendar were fast days – days on which people weren't supposed to eat meat, but could eat fish or cheese instead.

The banks of the River Thames were lined with wharves for ships to unload goods as well as the houses and warehouses of successful City merchants.

66 Up by water to Barne Elmes, where we walked by moonshine, ... and drank and had cold meat in the boat, and did eat, and sang ...99

Samuel Pepys, 21 July 1667

A Lord Mayor's water procession of the 1680s.

Outside the City's Walls

The River Fleet enters the Thames. Bridewell prison is on the left.

If you passed through the City of London's old walls at Ludgate and continued westwards down Ludgate Hill, you'd come to the River Fleet. This was the largest of the rivers that flowed through London into the Thames.

Filthy Fleet

The River Fleet rises on Hampstead Heath. In the 1660s part of the river flowed through open fields before reaching London's built-up area. Within London, the Fleet was surrounded by poor-quality housing. Residents treated it like an open sewer, filling the river with rubbish and filth. Several prisons were built near the Fleet, including Newgate, the Fleet and Bridewell.

Clerkenwell

To the north of the City lay Clerkenwell. Named after a medieval well, Clerkenwell grew up around a village green but the nearby City of London eventually swallowed it up. In the 1660s Clerkenwell was a fashionable place to live – Oliver Cromwell owned a house just off Clerkenwell Green.

Blackfriars and Bridewell

The Fleet entered the Thames at Blackfriars. This was a crowded district built around the site of a medieval monastery – the monks were known as the 'Black Friars'. Across the Fleet was Bridewell. This had originally been a palace belonging to Henry VIII but it was converted into a women's prison in the mid 1500s.

Fleet Street

This ancient street led from the River Fleet westwards, eventually becoming the Strand, which in turn led on to Charing Cross. Fleet Street had many small lanes built off it. These accessed 'courts', or small squares, were packed with housing.

Salisbury Court and its theatre

Just off Fleet Street was Salisbury Court, where Samuel Pepys was born. At the south end stood Salisbury Gardens Theatre, dating from 1629. This was the last London theatre to be opened before all theatres were closed by the Puritans in 1642 as they were thought to be immoral. However, secret performances continued at Salisbury Gardens until 1649, when government officials smashed up its interior. With the Restoration plays became popular again, and the theatre reopened. A new, bigger theatre, Dorset Gardens Theatre, was built further south in 1671.

Dorset Gardens Theatre.

Prince Henry's room

Number 17 Fleet Street (above) is one of the few buildings in this area of London to survive, and gives you a good idea of what much of London looked like. In the 1660s it was the Fountain Inn, and Samuel Pepys often stopped in here for a drink. The room known as 'Prince Henry's room' is on the first floor. It has a fine decorated plaster ceiling and City of London events are sometimes held there.

19

Throughout the early part of the 1600s, London expanded away from the historic crowded City, with its smells and narrow streets. Architects and builders created new areas with wide streets and fine houses let to wealthy tenants.

The architect Inigo Jones.

Lincoln's Inn Fields

This area was first built up in the 1630s when William Newton, one of London's first developers, was granted a licence to build houses around a square. These were in the Italian style, following the ideas of Inigo Jones (see right). Three storeys high, the buildings had attractive matching frontages.

 ## Covent Garden

Further west, north of the Strand, was Covent Garden, also developed in the 1630s. Here Jones designed an Italian-style open space, or piazza, surrounded by exclusive houses and a new church (see above). The houses were fronted by covered walkways so residents didn't get their fine clothes wet on rainy days.

Inigo Jones (1573-1652)

The son of a London clothmaker, Jones studied in Italy. He promoted the use of Classical architecture – the revived building styles of ancient Greece and Rome – which were only just beginning to be appreciated in England. Some of his most famous buildings, such as the Queen's House in Greenwich and the Banqueting House (see page 39) still stand today.

New Developments

Loos and poos

London houses in the 1660s, even posh new ones, didn't have flushing indoor lavatories. Most had a privy with a brick vault underneath, in which poo collected until it was dug out and removed by 'night-soil men' (so called because they worked after dark).

An 18th-century advert for night-soil man John Hunt.

Decline and revival

During the civil wars, Covent Garden fell on hard times. Shops were originally banned but from the early 1640s, illegal market traders selling fruit and vegetables moved in. In 1670 King Charles granted the Duke of Bedford permission to hold a market – this was to last more than 300 years.

The Theatre Royal

The new Theatre Royal Covent Garden opened on 7 May 1663. If you went to a performance you'd sit in rising rows of seats, like a theatre today. Cheap seats were still in the pit, as they had been in Shakespeare's time. The actress Nell Gwyn, one of King Charles' girlfriends, began her career selling oranges in the Theatre Royal.

A performance at the Theatre Royal.

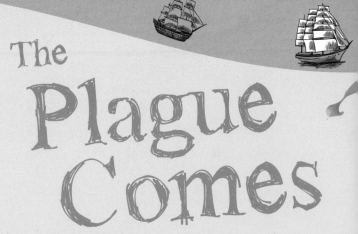

In April 1665 a young woman was buried in the churchyard of St Paul's Church, Covent Garden. The cause of her death was familiar – bubonic plague. No one could have suspected that this was the beginning of one of the worst epidemics of the disease in London's history.

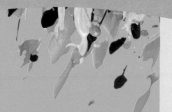

The Plague Comes

What was it?

Bubonic plague is a disease caused by the bacterium *yersinia pestis*. It causes severe, painful swellings in the armpits and groin (the 'buboes' of the disease's name), fever and, in most cases, death in four or five days. Today doctors treat plague with antibiotics, which were discovered in 1928.

> 66 This day, much against my will, I did in Drury Lane see two or three houses marked with a red cross upon the doors, and "Lord have mercy upon us" writ there; which was a sad sight to me. 99
>
> Samuel Pepys, 7 June 1665

Plague sufferers shut in a room. One person, already dead, is laid out for burial.

Fleas and rats

Fleas bite mammals to suck their blood for food. Plague was spread by infected fleas living on black rats (left), which were everywhere in 1660s London. When the rodents died, the infected fleas looked for new hosts. This usually meant biting a nearby human, who then became ill.

A London street during the plague. A cart collects dead bodies while a fire has been lit to purify the air.

Causes unknown

In the 1660s, the origin of plague was a mystery. There were many theories. Some thought that the outbreak was caused by such things as 'bad air', and sniffed sweet-smelling herbs or burned pots of sulphur to purify the atmosphere. However, none of these remedies worked and the disease spread like wildfire. Those who could fled from London (below) to relatives in the countryside. King Charles and his court moved to Oxford.

Shutting up the sick

Faced with a nightmare, London's authorities did what they could. When a case was reported by the parish 'searchers' – workers employed to look for cases of plague – the house was sealed. Officials painted a red cross on the front door with the words LORD HAVE MERCY UPON US written underneath. These measures were supposed to contain the disease. But with the sick and the well confined together, uninfected persons soon became ill.

Lord have Mercy upon Us!

Daniel Defoe published his *Journal of the Plague Year* many years after the epidemic. The book tells the story of a fictional Londoner living through the plague. Here he describes one of the pits:

"But now, at the beginning of September, the plague raging in a dreadful manner, and the number of burials in our parish increasing to more than was ever buried in any parish about London of no larger extent, they ordered this dreadful gulf to be dug – for such it was, rather than a pit.

They had supposed this pit would have supplied them for a month or more when they dug it ... (but) ... the pit being finished the 4th of September, I think, they began to bury in it the 6th, and by the 20th, which was just two weeks, they had thrown into it 1,114 bodies ..."

By September cases of the plague had increased terrifyingly, killing thousands each week. The City of London, with its crowded housing, was badly affected. Death was everywhere and people became convinced that the end of the world had come.

Plague pits

With so many to bury, parishes began to dig huge 'plague pits' to accommodate all the bodies. You would have seen carts loaded with bodies rumbling through the streets after dark, collecting corpses by torch- or lantern-light.

A new twist

As the epidemic went on, something strange began to happen – some victims began to die much more quickly. You could be well one day and dead just two days later. This is because, over time, bubonic plague mutates (changes) into much more deadly forms.

Death – personified as a huge skeleton – conquers London. On the left, victims covered with sores lie down to die. On the right, Londoners escaping the plague are refused entry to other towns.

Plague victims are buried.

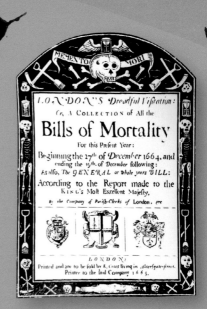

The Bills of Mortality for 1665.

Keeping track of the dead

Within the City of London, the Worshipful Company of Parish Clerks dutifully kept records of births and deaths. The 'Bills of Mortality' listed how many people died every week and of what causes. At the end of 1665 all the Bills of Mortality for the year were published. The title page, shown here, is decorated with nightmare pictures including skulls, skeletons and, at the bottom, a corpse wrapped in a winding sheet.

The plague finally subsides

By the time cold winter weather arrived in December 1665 the epidemic was finally on the wane, but more than 100,000 people had died. Those who had fled earlier in the year – including the King and his court – began to drift back to London. Here, victims who had recovered had acquired an immunity to the disease; the rest had been shovelled into mass graves.

A Fire in Pudding Lane

The next summer, 1666, was hot and dry. The City of London sweltered in heat. Late on the evening of Saturday 1 September, baker Thomas Farrinor shut down the oven at his house in Pudding Lane, near St Magnus Church and went to bed. But he missed one red-hot ember. By the time Farrinor was awakened by his servant the house was ablaze. Sparks landed on nearby buildings and soon they too were on fir The Great Fire of London had begun.

Not uncommon

In the 1600s fires in towns and cities were common. People usually managed to put them out with only a few houses lost. Really big fires, such as the one that destroyed most of Dorchester in 1613, remained a terrifying memory for years.

Not much to worry about

At first, people living distant from the fire thought that it was just another small outbreak. When the Lord Mayor, Sir Thomas Bludworth, was told of the fire he took a look and is reputed to have said that "... a woman might piss it out".

> 66 Jane (the Pepys' maid) called us up about three in the morning, to tell us of a great fire they saw in the City. So I rose and slipped on my nightgowne, and went to her window, and thought it ... far enough off; and so went to bed again and to sleep. 99

Samuel Pepys, describing his reaction to the start of the Great Fire (he lived near the Tower of London)

A reconstruction of Pudding Lane on the night of the fire.

Leather firefighting bucket from the 1600s.

The fire spreads

But timber-framed houses catch fire easily: the Pudding Lane fire spread quickly in the dry conditions. Soon entire streets were ablaze. The Lord Mayor should have ordered the pulling down of houses, the most effective way of containing fire, but people resisted as it meant destroying their property. Had you been in the streets the next day you would have seen hot embers and sparks jumping up the narrow smoke-filled lanes, carried on the strong east wind.

Warehouses go up

By Sunday morning the fire reached nearby Thames Street. Its riverside warehouses were full of flammable oil, alcohol and tar. The resulting explosions created a firestorm, spreading the blaze even faster. By now the fire really was out of control.

Londoners crowd under London Bridge to escape the fire in this 17th-century painting.

27

Pepys' account

Throughout Sunday the fire spread all along the river. Samuel Pepys went out in a boat to see what was going on. He recorded:

"Everybody endeavouring to remove their goods, and flinging (them) into the river or bringing them into lighters that lay off; poor people staying in their houses as long as till the very fire touched them, and then running into boats ...

And among other things, the poor pigeons, I perceive, were loth to leave their houses, but hovered about the windows and balconies, till they some of them burned their wings and fell down."

" Having stayed, and in an hour's time seen the fire rage every way, and nobody, to my sight, endeavouring to quench it, but to remove their goods, and leave all to the fire ... "

No water

Some areas of the City had a basic water supply carried in wooden pipes (see pages 12-13). When desperate Londoners bored holes in the pipes to try and obtain water to quench fires in their own areas, the water pressure in the rest of the pipes was reduced to a trickle.

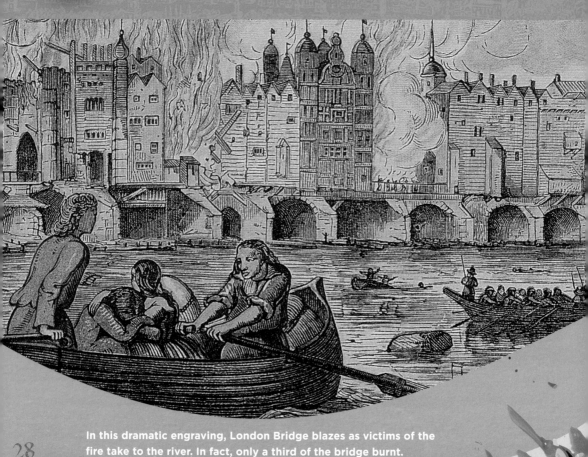

In this dramatic engraving, London Bridge blazes as victims of the fire take to the river. In fact, only a third of the bridge burnt.

Telling the King

Pepys hurried to Whitehall Palace on Sunday to tell King Charles about the disaster. The King commanded Pepys to find the Lord Mayor and order him to demolish houses. Pepys eventually caught up with Bludworth, the Lord Mayor, in Cannon Street, now choked with fleeing, terrified Londoners:

"To the King's message he (Bludworth) cried, like a fainting woman, 'Lord! what can I do? I am spent: people will not obey me. I have been pulling down houses; but the fire overtakes us faster than we can do it."

Royals take charge

King Charles took direct action on Monday, putting his brother James, the Duke of York, in charge. The Duke posted groups of more than 100 soldiers and firefighters around the City in the path of the fire. An official with the power to order houses to be torn down commanded each group. Charles himself rode on horseback between the groups. He handed out gold coins to encourage the firefighters and personally helped fight some of the flames.

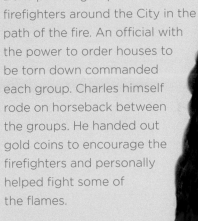

James, Duke of York, King Charles II's younger brother.

Moving fast

On Monday the fire blazed north through the City of London. Stone-built churches and livery company halls alike were quickly gutted. By the afternoon the flames reached the Royal Exchange, which was reduced to ashes in hours. Even at this stage many wealthy City merchants, worried about losing their valuable property, refused to allow any houses to be torn down to create firebreaks.

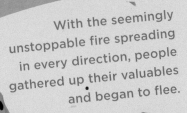

With the seemingly unstoppable fire spreading in every direction, people gathered up their valuables and began to flee.

A City Ablaze

The Fire Rages On

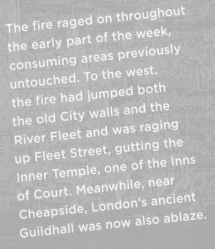

The fire raged on throughout the early part of the week, consuming areas previously untouched. To the west, the fire had jumped both the old City walls and the River Fleet and was raging up Fleet Street, gutting the Inner Temple, one of the Inns of Court. Meanwhile, near Cheapside, London's ancient Guildhall was now also ablaze.

Leaving the City

Samuel Pepys packed up his valuables, ready to carry them to safety:

"About four o'clock in the morning, my Lady Batten sent me a cart to carry away all my money, and plate (silver), and best things, to Sir W. Rider's at Bethnal Green. Which I did riding myself in my nightgown in the cart; and, Lord! to see how the streets and the highways are crowded with people running and riding, and getting of carts at any rate to fetch away things."

St Paul's goes up

St Paul's Cathedral caught fire late on Tuesday, and in hours was a roofless ruin. The acres of lead covering its roof melted from the extreme heat, rolling down the walls in a red-hot torrent. When blazing roof timbers crashed down they set fire to thousands of printed books stored in the crypt (cellar) by the Worshipful Company of Stationers.

Pepys buries a cheese

Pepys, having returned from Bethnal Green, looked around for other ways to save his possessions. He and his neighbours came up with the idea of burying them:

"Sir W. Batten not knowing how to remove his wine, did dig a pit in the garden, and laid it in there; and I took the opportunity of laying all the papers of my office that I could not otherwise dispose of. And in the evening Sir W. Pen and I did dig another, and put our wine in it; and I my Parmazan cheese, as well as some other things."

Demolition starts to work

On Tuesday the organised tearing down of houses was finally underway. The Duke of York commanded hundreds of sailors from the docks to the east of London to come and help. They brought gunpowder with them and soon whole streets of houses were blown up, creating wide firebreaks.

A glimmer of hope

Late on Tuesday the east wind, which had been vital in spreading the fire, rose then fell and changed direction. Red-hot embers were now blown back onto areas that had already been burnt, and the fire began to subside. By Wednesday evening the spread of the fire had finally been stopped.

17th-century firefighters used hooks on poles to demolish houses.

Refugees

The open space of Moorfields, just north of the City walls, was packed with people who had fled their burning homes and had set up a huge refugee camp. King Charles addressed them on Thursday, promising them handouts of money. He was also keen to stop rumours that the Fire had been started by Roman Catholics or the Dutch, with whom England was at war.

The City ablaze at the height of the Great Fire.

Old St Paul's after the fire – a roofless, smoking ruin.

> 66 I went this morning on foot from Whitehall as far as London Bridge ... with extraordinary difficulty, clambering over heaps of yet smoking rubbish, and frequently mistaking where I was. The ground under my feet so hot, that it even burnt the soles of my shoes ... The people who now walked about the ruins appeared like men in some dismal desert, or rather in some great city laid waste by a cruel enemy ...
>
> *John Evelyn, diarist*

After the Fire

After the flames finally died down, five-sixths of the City of London was a smoking ruin. Rebuilding was needed quickly so that business could carry on – but the scale of the work was massive.

Helping those affected

Even before the flames were put out, King Charles issued a 'Royal Proclamation for Relief'. This authorised money to be collected in churches all over the country to help Londoners who had lost their homes. People gave generously because at another time it could be their town or city that went up in flames.

Rebuilding begins

Rebuilding London began in April 1667. Property owners first had to clear their plots of debris so the ground could be surveyed. New buildings had to be made of brick and stone. City officials realised that not all property owners could afford to rebuild at once, but regulations insisted that all the buildings eventually had to look the same.

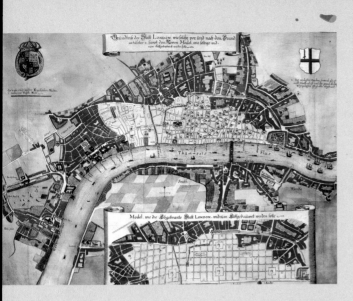

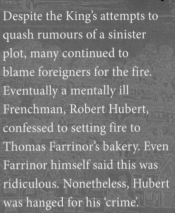

Scapegoat

Despite the King's attempts to quash rumours of a sinister plot, many continued to blame foreigners for the fire. Eventually a mentally ill Frenchman, Robert Hubert, confessed to setting fire to Thomas Farrinor's bakery. Even Farrinor himself said this was ridiculous. Nonetheless, Hubert was hanged for his 'crime'.

Touring the ruins

This map of London by artist Wenceslaus Hollar shows just how much of the City was destroyed. The pink portion indicates the burnt areas. St Paul's, the Royal Exchange and many other key buildings and churches were in ruins.

Plans for new St Paul's.

Radical plans

Some thinkers and architects, such as Christopher Wren (see page 15), saw the Great Fire as an unmissable chance to build a modern city. Wren wanted to replace London's higgledy-piggledy network of medieval streets and lanes with something more logical. But in the end his plans were unworkable – there were simply too many property owners to deal with.

Wren's radical plans for rebuilding St Paul's with a huge dome were approved, however, and the new cathedral was eventually completed in 1709. In the meantime, many of the City's gutted parish churches and other buildings, including the front of the Guildhall, were rebuilt to Wren's designs.

Christopher Wren, painted by John Closterman, 1690.

London Bridge had existed as London's only road crossing of the river since the late 1100s. Lined with houses and shops, it was one of the wonders of its age.

The bridge and the Great Fire

Only about one-third of the buildings on the bridge were burnt in the Great Fire. That all of the bridge didn't burn was due to an earlier fire in 1633, when many of the houses near the north end of the bridge went up in flames. Some of these hadn't been rebuilt by 1666. This gap created a firebreak, stopping the Great Fire from spreading along the entire length of the bridge.

Nonsuch House

This amazing building was prefabricated in the Netherlands in the 1500s. It was shipped to London and erected at the centre of the bridge, held together with wooden pegs. Nonsuch House was beautifully decorated with elaborate paintwork, windows and carving, had two sundials to tell people the time and four domed turrets.

Arches and rapids

London Bridge's 19 arches rested on 'starlings' – foundations sunk into the riverbed. The starlings created a build up of water, resulting in rapids. Passing through the arches in a boat was known as 'shooting the bridge' and was dangerous work.

Old London Bridge

Crossing the river

Had you wanted to make the 350-m-long river crossing you would have experienced a slow dark journey. The buildings on either side of the bridge were up to seven storeys high, and this blocked out much of the light. The 4-m-wide roadway itself was so jammed with traffic going to and from the south side of the river that a crossing could take up to an hour.

Thames watermen

Thames watermen were the cab drivers of 1660s London. They rowed small boats called wherries, taking passengers up and down the river for money. With City streets so crowded, going by boat was usually the fastest way to get somewhere. Passengers often complained that they were overcharged by the watermen, and that they were a rowdy and rude lot.

The Stone Gate

Standing near the southern end of the bridge, this gate could be closed to shut off the bridge to invaders from the south. On top of the gate were displayed up to 30 rotting human heads and other body parts, stuck on pikes. These were the remains of traitors who had been hanged, drawn and quartered (see page 10).

Southwark and Bankside

Leaving the burnt City behind you and making the slow, crowded crossing of London Bridge, you would find yourself in Southwark. Here, busy streets surrounded the Borough, with its many taverns and inns. Nearby were the rowdy entertainments of Bankside.

St Saviour's

This large Gothic church was originally known as St Mary Overie, which meant 'St Mary over the water', or 'across the river from the City'. It became St Saviour's in the 1530s and in the 1660s was the parish church of the Southwark area. William Shakespeare's brother, Edmund, was buried here in 1607.

Winchester Palace

Walking west along the Thames, with the dank smell of the river in your nose, you'd arrive at this huge complex. Dating from medieval times, the palace was originally the London home of the Bishop of Winchester. Once magnificent, by the 1660s the palace had been converted into shabby flats and crumbling warehouses. During the civil wars prisoners had been kept here.

St Saviour's Church was enlarged to become today's Southwark Cathedral, shown here.

" saw some good sport of the bull's tossing of the dogs: one into the very boxes. But it is a very rude and nasty pleasure. "

Samuel Pepys, 14 August 1666

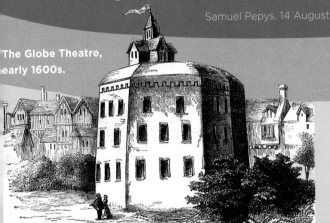

The Globe Theatre, early 1600s.

Holland's Leaguer looked like a fortified manor house.

Liberty of the Clink

Part of Bankside was known as the 'Liberty of the Clink', and was outside the control of the City of London. This meant that the area became home to illegal traders, criminals, drinking dens, pleasure gardens, gambling houses and theatres.

The Globe Theatre flourished on Bankside earlier in the 1600s, but had closed in 1642. It is famous for being the theatre where many of William Shakespeare's plays were performed.

Bull and bear baiting

These cruel sports were popular on Bankside, and drew huge crowds. Bulls or bears were chained to posts and attacked by large dogs. People bet money on which animal would win. The fights left the animals badly maimed, and they often bled to death.

Bankside pleasures

'Places of resort' flourished in the free and easy atmosphere of Bankside. Londoners came here to eat and drink, watch bull and bear baiting, gamble and conduct romantic affairs. They often had fanciful-sounding names. 'Holland's Leaguer' and 'Paris Garden' were two of the most famous. A picture of Holland's Leaguer dating from the 1600s shows a fine building surrounded by a moat with a fortified gateway and a guard posted to keep snoopers out.

The sport of bear baiting was both cruel and dangerous.

Whitehall Palace

Situated on the banks of the River Thames between Westminster and Charing Cross, Whitehall Palace had been the main residence of English monarchs since the 1530s.

A palace of many parts

Whitehall Palace was made up of many interconnected parts, containing gardens, courtyards, galleries, kitchens, a chapel, a great hall and storage areas. Two public roads cut right through the palace. With more than 1,500 rooms, the palace was the largest secular (non-church) complex of buildings in England.

Charles II and the palace

King Charles made a lot of improvements to Whitehall – during his reign he rebuilt his own and the Queen's apartments. He also added further sets of rooms for his many girlfriends. But the money voted by Parliament to pay for the King and his court was never enough to allow Charles to fulfil all his plans.

The Banqueting House

Charles's grandfather, King James I, commissioned Inigo Jones to design this beautiful building in 1622. James wanted a place in which to hold masques – court entertainments in which costumed players and musicians performed in front of elaborate theatrical sets. The magnificent ceiling of the Banqueting House was decorated by the Flemish artist Peter Paul Rubens. It was outside the Banqueting House, on a scaffold erected at first-floor level, that Charles II's father, King Charles I, was beheaded in 1649.

The painted ceiling of the Banqueting House.

A 17th-century view of Whitehall Palace from St James's Park. The Banqueting House is the tallest building on the left.

The Royal Society

With Charles's restoration came a new interest in science. This scientific organisation was founded by a group of doctors and thinkers in November 1660. For many years it met at Gresham College in the City of London. Here you might have attended a scientific lecture or the dissection of a hanged criminal, whose bodies were allowed by law to be used for experiments.

A walk in the garden

Had you been able to gain access to the palace you might have seen Charles walking in the Privy (private) Garden. He and his courtiers would have been wearing colourful, expensive silk clothes cut in the latest French fashion as they 'took the air' on its gravel paths.

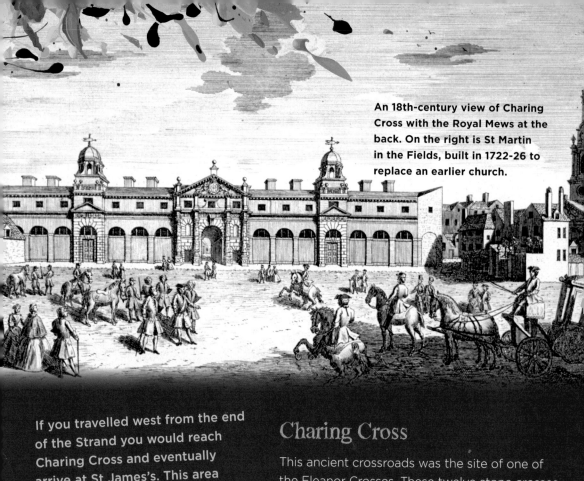

An 18th-century view of Charing Cross with the Royal Mews at the back. On the right is St Martin in the Fields, built in 1722-26 to replace an earlier church.

If you travelled west from the end of the Strand you would reach Charing Cross and eventually arrive at St James's. This area of London was fast becoming fashionable in the 1660s, helped by King Charles's love of walking in the park – and a ball game.

Charing Cross

This ancient crossroads was the site of one of the Eleanor Crosses. These twelve stone crosses were built by King Edward I in the 1290s to mark the nightly resting places of the body of his dead queen, Eleanor, on the journey from Lincolnshire to her burial in Westminster Abbey. In the 1660s the Royal Mews, (stables) were located at Charing Cross, on the site of what is today Trafalgar Square.

Fashionable St James's

Developing St James's

Development of St James's really got underway at the Restoration. In 1665 Charles II granted his friend Henry Jermyn, Earl of St Albans, land that would become St James's Square, with permission to build houses to rent out to wealthy tenants.

St James's Palace

St James's Palace dated from the 1530s. During the civil wars it had been used as a military prison, where soldiers loyal to King Charles I were kept in horrid conditions. After the Restoration Charles II renovated the palace and built a chapel for his Roman Catholic queen, Catherine of Braganza.

Pall Mall

This wide street was originally the playing ground for a French game, *paille maille*. This was like a combination of golf and croquet – players hit balls through hoops with mallets. It was played on a pitch made of crushed cockleshells.

The game of *paille maille*.

> 66 So I into St James's Park, where I saw the Duke of York playing at paille maille, the first time that ever I saw the sport. 99
>
> Samuel Pepys, 2 April 1661

St James's Park

This park dated from the time of King James I. However it had been neglected under Cromwell's rule, when many of its trees were chopped down for firewood. Charles II restored the park, converting its slimy ponds into a wide canal and stocking it with wild birds, including Canada geese. If you went for a walk there you might see the King and even speak with him, as Charles often stopped to chat with ordinary people.

The lake in St James's Park.

Parliament

Parlament Houfe

the Hall

A royal palace and abbey had existed at Westminster since the 1000s. The surrounding area had grown up to supply the needs of the people living and working there. By the 1660s Westminster was the City of London's 'far west' cousin.

The Great Seal of Cromwell's Commonwealth government shows MPs in the House of Commons in the 1650s.

Parliament

In the 1660s Parliament met at Westminster, just as it does today. The House of Lords met in the Queen's Chamber, a small medieval hall, while the House of Commons assembled in St Stephen's Chapel. The layout of the modern House of Commons takes its form from this medieval religious building. Instead of a priest at the front there sits the Speaker. Members of Parliament sit on benches arranged longways, just as the seats would have been in the old chapel – and still are in many Oxford and Cambridge colleges.

d Westminster

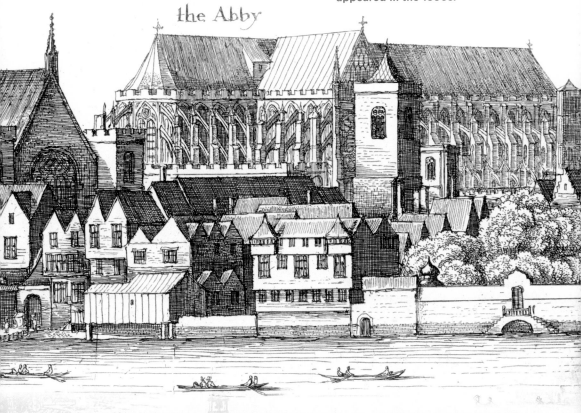

The Houses of Parliament, Westminster Hall and Westminster Abbey as they appeared in the 1660s.

the Abby

Palace of Westminster

This ancient riverside royal palace had been the main residence of the monarch until 1512, when a fire destroyed the royal apartments. In the 1660s the country's main law courts met in Westminster Hall (right), with its beautiful medieval roof. Here up to three courts were in session at once, so the hall must have been filled with a confusing babble of voices.

The Abbey

Founded in 960, Westminster Abbey became the site of royal coronations, funerals and burials. In the 1660s you could visit the Abbey to see the tombs of kings and queens, just as Samuel Pepys did. But the building would have looked different – the two tall western towers weren't built until the 1720s.

London Goes West

By the end of the 1660s and into the 1670s London was growing rapidly westwards. The peace and prosperity brought by the Restoration, along with the profits of foreign trade, turned previously undeveloped areas of the capital into a maze of streets and squares.

Soho Square, one of the new look West End squares.

The City rebuilt

Over the next 50 years the burnt parts of the City of London were rebuilt in brick and stone. These materials produced elegant streets influenced by Classical architecture.

Areas west of the City and north of the Strand that had until recently been green fields were now rapidly built up. These included Holborn, Bloomsbury, St Giles, Leicester Square and Soho. Building regulations decreed that new houses in these areas had to be made of brick, so millions of bricks poured into London from brick-making kilns in the fields outside the capital.

This 18th-century Bloomsbury terrace follows the pattern of houses built around a square established after the Great Fire.

Speculative building

Most of the land available for development was owned by aristocrats such as the Earl of Southampton. He began to develop his Bloomsbury estate in the mid 1660s. These wealthy people subdivided their land into building plots. These were leased to 'speculative builders'. The builders constructed houses on the plots and collected annual rents from tenants, making a fortune in the process. When the leases eventually expired, the houses built became the property of the original landowner. Much of the West End of London was to be built up in this way.

Nicholas Barbon: speculative builder

The son of a Puritan preacher, Nicholas was christened Nicholas If-Jesus-Christ-Had-Not-Died-For-Thee-Thou-Hadst-Been-Damned. Born in the late 1630s, Barbon first qualified as a doctor. However, as London expanded he was quick to spot opportunities to make money, and developed many streets round the Strand and Bloomsbury. A pioneer of both fire insurance and banking, Barbon helped to found a bank that loaned money against the value of property in a similar way to modern mortgages. He eventually became an MP and died a very wealthy man in 1698.

London on fire

So a new London emerged from the ashes of the Great Fire but the optimism of the Restoration period lit a different kind of fire – a blaze of ideas and possibilities that catapulted London into the modern age. Institutions such as the Royal Society promoted science. The new systems of banking financed expeditions that traded around the world, backed up by a strong and efficient Royal Navy (developed by people like Samuel Pepys). Within 100 years Britain became a world power. At the heart of all this activity was rebuilt London. Catastrophic events such as the Great Fire, the Blitz of the Second World War (1939–45) or the terrorist bombings of 2005 remind us of London's greatest strength: like the phoenix, its ability to overcome disaster and to rise again.

St Paul's Cathedral today.

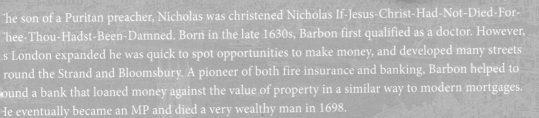

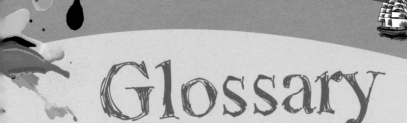

Glossary

Anglican – part of the Church of England.

Architect – a person who designs buildings.

Bishop – in the Church of England and the Roman Catholic Church, a senior priest in charge of a diocese.

Bubonic plague – a deadly disease caused by the bacterium *yersinia pestis*. Today it can be treated with antibiotics.

Church of England – the Church founded by King Henry VIII in 1534–36 when he no longer acknowledged the religious authority of the Pope in Rome.

City of London – the historic heart of London that lies inside the original medieval walled city (some of which dates back to Roman times).

Civil servant – a person employed by the government to administer its laws.

Civil war – when citizens of the same country fight each other in armed conflict.

Classical – in architecture, the building styles of ancient Greece and Rome.

Commonwealth of England – the period after the English civil wars, 1649-1660, when England and Wales (and later Scotland and Ireland) were ruled by Parliament without a king.

Coronation – the ceremony that officially creates a king or queen.

Court, the – a monarch and all his or her trusted advisers, servants and staff.

Courtier – a person who serves a monarch at court.

Developer – a person or company that builds up part of a city with new houses.

Diocese – the area for which a bishop is responsible. At its heart is a cathedral.

Firebreak – an area of waste ground created to stop an oncoming fire by robbing it of fuel.

Flammable – easily set alight.

Guild – in the City of London, an organisation responsible for regulating a particular trade and promoting the welfare of its members. Also known as a livery company.

Guildhall – the centre of government for the City of London.

Lighters – a small, flat-bottomed boat used to transport goods, often from larger ships to land.

Livery company – see Guild.

Lord Mayor – the elected head of government for the City of London.

Parish – the smallest area within the Church of England or the Roman Catholic Church. At its heart is the local church building.

Parliament – refers to people who meet in and the buildings that hold the House of Lords and House of Commons where British law is made.

Protestant – a member of any of the Western Christian Churches who are separate from the Roman Catholic Church in ways that link back to the Reformation of the 16th century, or relating to these churches.

Puritans – in the 1500s and 1600s, a group of people within the Church of England who were very religious and believed strongly that reading the Bible and listening to sermons were the most important things in Christian life.

Restoration – when Charles II returned from exile in the Netherlands in 1660 to take his place as king after the brief era of the Commonwealth.

Roman Catholic – a Christian who acknowledges the religious authority of the Pope in Rome.

Sermon – a religious speech delivered by a priest or minister.

Speculative builder – in the late 1600s, someone who built houses to let to tenants on land leased by a landowner.

Traitor – someone convicted of plotting against or attempting to overthrow a king, queen or government.

Wharf – a platform built on a riverbank, which is level with the boats, making it easy to load and unload them.

Wherry – in the 1600s, a small Thames boat rowed by a waterman and for hire like a taxi.

Places to visit

Walk the streets of London and you will find plenty of the places mentioned in this book.

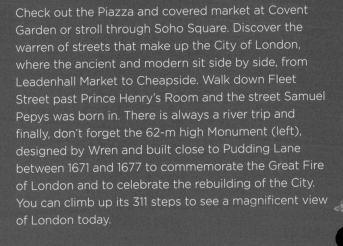

Check out the Piazza and covered market at Covent Garden or stroll through Soho Square. Discover the warren of streets that make up the City of London, where the ancient and modern sit side by side, from Leadenhall Market to Cheapside. Walk down Fleet Street past Prince Henry's Room and the street Samuel Pepys was born in. There is always a river trip and finally, don't forget the 62-m high Monument (left), designed by Wren and built close to Pudding Lane between 1671 and 1677 to commemorate the Great Fire of London and to celebrate the rebuilding of the City. You can climb up its 311 steps to see a magnificent view of London today.

Find out more details to plan your visit on the websites given here.

The Banqueting House
www.hrp.org.uk/BanquetingHouse

Guildhall
www.guildhall.cityoflondon.gov.uk

The National Portrait Gallery
www.npg.org.uk

The Monument to the Great Fire of London
www.themonument.info/

Museum of London
www.museumoflondon.org.uk

Museum of London Docklands
www.museumoflondon.org.uk/docklands/

St Paul's Cathedral
www.stpauls.co.uk

St Saviour's – now Southwark Cathedral
cathedral.southwark.anglican.org

The Tower of London
www.hrp.org.uk/TowerOfLondon

Worshipful Company of Watermen and Lightermen
watermenscompany.com/

Index

Franklin Watts
Published in Great Britain
in paperback in 2018 by
The Watts Publishing
Group

Copyright © The Watts
Publishing Group, 2016

All rights reserved.

Credits
Editor: Rachel Cooke
Cover design:
Peter Scoulding
Designer: Jennie Child
based on a concept
by Jennifer Rose
Picture researcher: Diana
Morris

MIX
Paper from
responsible sources
FSC® C104740

Picture credits:
Antiquarian Images/Mary Evans PL: 33tl. Art/Shutterstock:
44t. Brooke Becker/Shutterstock: 40c. bikeworldtravel/
Shutterstock: 47. The British Library Board: 04-05.
cheeseherbs/Shutterstock: 7tl. corund/Shutterstock: 16bl.
© Crown Copyright. Government Art Collection: 38-39.
dani3315/Shutterstock: 25c. Mary Evans PL: 29t. Mary
Evans PL/Alamy: 42tl. Everett Historical/Shutterstock:
37cl. Falkenstein/Alamy: 18t. Evgenia Fashayan/
Shutterstock: 16tr. Fine Art Images/HIP/Topfoto: 23t.
Dragana Gerasimoski/Shutterstock: 20br. Brian Giff/
Shutterstock: 7c. Andrii Gorulko/Shutterstock: 13t. The
Granger Collection/Topfoto: 24t. Jonny Greig/Alamy: 12b.
Iri Gri/Shutterstock: 30c. Guildhall Library and Art Gallery/
Alamy: 18b. Guildhall Library and Art Gallery/Getty Images:
40t. Gutenburg Project: 15t. HIP/Topfoto: 7b. Vitalii Hulai/
Shutterstock: 22b. Hulton Archive/Getty Images: 10bl.
Igoror/Shutterstock: 23c. Interfoto/Alamy: 26c. Val-Iva/
Shutterstock: 18c. Jiunn/Shutterstock: 19tl. Kensii991/
Shutterstock: 20cl. Kovalevska/Shutterstock: 17t. La
Garda/Shutterstock: 26t. Library of Congress: 2-3,16-17c,
20tl. Liszt Collection/Topfoto: 27b. London Fire Brigade/
Mary Evans PL: 31b. London Metropolitan Archives, City
of London/BAL: 30t, 32t. Fernando Camiel Machado/
Dreamstime: 5tl. Morphant Creation/Shutterstock: 37t.
David Muscroft/Shutterstock: 6tl. Museum of London:
27c. Museum of London/Art Archive: 6c. Nature Art/
Shutterstock: 33tr. Hein Nouwens/Shutterstock: 41c, 41b.
olegtoka/Shutterstock: 19b. paket/Shutterstock: 36t.
Photogènes: 5tr, 10tl, 10tr,19tr, 27tr, 37b, 41t, 41bc, 43b,
45tl, 45b. Photo Researchers/Mary Evans PL: 28b. Private
Collection/Bridgeman Art Library: 8b, 33b, 44b. Pudding
Lane Productions: 27tl. radmilla75/Shutterstock:
45tr. Viktorija Reuta/Shutterstock:21c, 32c. Yulia
Reznikov/Shutterstock: 9tl. Royal Collection
Trust/© Her Majesty Queen Elizabeth II, 2016:
17b. Alex Roz/Shutterstock: 45c. Science
Museum: 28c. Martin Spurny/Shutterstock:
8t, 9br. Sheila Terry/SPL: 22c. Irina Tischenko/
Shutterstock: 33cl. Tupungato/Shutterstock:
36b. cc wikimedia commons: 9tr, 11tr, 11br, 12t,
13b, 14t, 15b, 20tr, 21tl, 21tr, 21b, 23b, 25t, 25b,
29b, 31t, 33cr, 34-35, 37cr, 39t, 42b.

Every attempt has been made to clear
copyright. Should there be any inadvertent
omission please apply to the publisher for
rectification.

ISBN 978 1 4451 6355 0
Library ebook ISBN 978 1 4451 4693 5
Printed in China.

Franklin Watts
An imprint of
Hachette Children's Group
Part of The Watts Publishing Group
Carmelite House
50 Victoria Embankment
London EC4Y 0DZ

An Hachette UK Company
www.hachette.co.uk

www.franklinwatts.co.uk